At the Park

FIRST EDITION
Series Editor Deborah Lock; **Designer** Sadie Thomas; **US Editor** Elizabeth Hester;
Production Alison Lenane; **DTP Designer** Almudena Díaz; **Jacket Designer** Simon Oon;
Reading Consultant Linda Gambrell, PhD

THIS EDITION
Editorial Management by Oriel Square
Produced for DK by WonderLab Group LLC
Jennifer Emmett, Erica Green, Kate Hale, *Founders*

Editors Grace Hill Smith, Libby Romero, Michaela Weglinski;
Photography Editors Kelley Miller, Annette Kiesow, Nicole DiMella;
Managing Editor Rachel Houghton; **Designers** Project Design Company;
Researcher Michelle Harris; **Copy Editor** Lori Merritt; **Indexer** Connie Binder; **Proofreader** Larry Shea;
Reading Specialist Dr. Jennifer Albro; **Curriculum Specialist** Elaine Larson

Published in the United States by DK Publishing
1745 Broadway, 20th Floor, New York, NY 10019

Copyright © 2023 Dorling Kindersley Limited
DK, a Division of Penguin Random House LLC
23 24 25 26 27 10 9 8 7 6 5 4 3 2 1
001–333430–Apr/2023

All rights reserved.
Without limiting the rights under the copyright reserved above, no part of this publication may be reproduced, stored in or introduced into a retrieval system, or transmitted, in any form, or by any means (electronic, mechanical, photocopying, recording, or otherwise), without the prior written permission of the copyright owner.
Published in Great Britain by Dorling Kindersley Limited

A catalog record for this book
is available from the Library of Congress.
HC ISBN: 978-0-7440-6688-3
PB ISBN: 978-0-7440-6689-0

DK books are available at special discounts when purchased in bulk for sales promotions, premiums, fundraising, or educational use. For details, contact: DK Publishing Special Markets, 1745 Broadway, 20th Floor, New York, NY 10019
SpecialSales@dk.com

Printed and bound in China

The publisher would like to thank the following for their kind permission to reproduce their images:
a=above; c=center; b=below; l=left; r=right; t=top; b/g=background
Alamy Stock Photo: Zoonar GmbH / amnuai butala 17bl; **Dreamstime.com:** Parawat Isarangura Na Ayudhaya 19bc, Irusik48 22bl, Weerapat Kiatdumrong 22br, 31tl, Sergey Novikov 24-25, Pioneer111 16bl, 19bl, 23bl, 23bc, Sergiy1975 23br, Zurijeta 30; **Getty Images:** DigitalVision / Yuji Kotani 23c; **Shutterstock.com:** Pascal Huot 12t, IrinaK 29bc, Anatoliy Karlyuk 27br, kdshutterman 27bc, Maya Kruchankova 27bl, Sergiy Kuzmin 17br, Christin Lola 10-11, Boris Medvedev 16br, Sergey Novikov 19c, Cheryl-Annette Parker 18bl, 31bl, SARAPON 16-17, stockphoto-graf 6br, 7b
Cover images: *Front:* **Dreamstime.com:** Batsugraphic tl, Natalia Nesterenko b, Dmitry Rogatnev;
Back: **Dreamstime.com:** Dmitry Rogatnev cla, cra
All other images © Dorling Kindersley

For the curious
www.dk.com

At the Park

Dawn Sirett

We like going to the park.

grass

 **balls**

We kick balls across the grass.

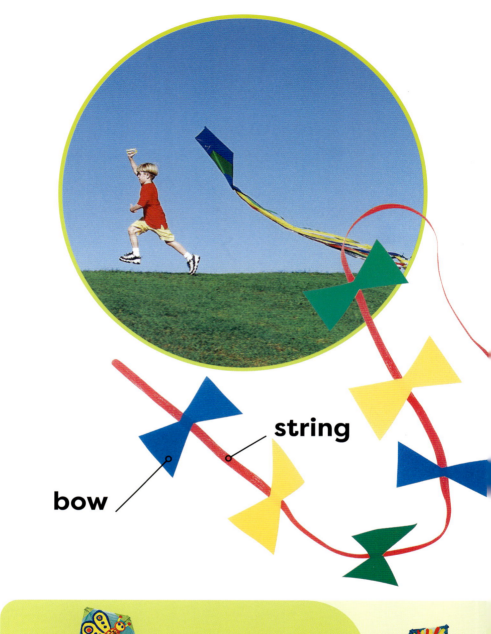

string

bow

 kites

We fly kites in the sky.

We play baseball with bats and balls.

baseball

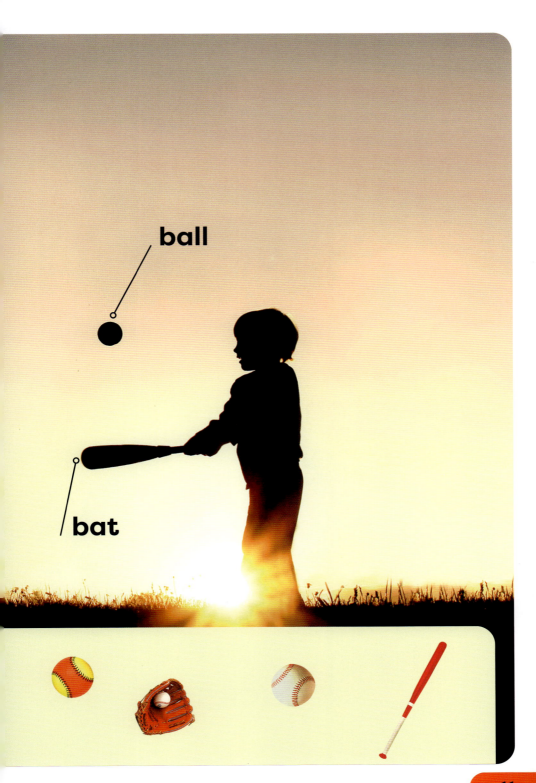

We watch ducks on the pond.

ducks

We sail boats on the water.

 **boats**

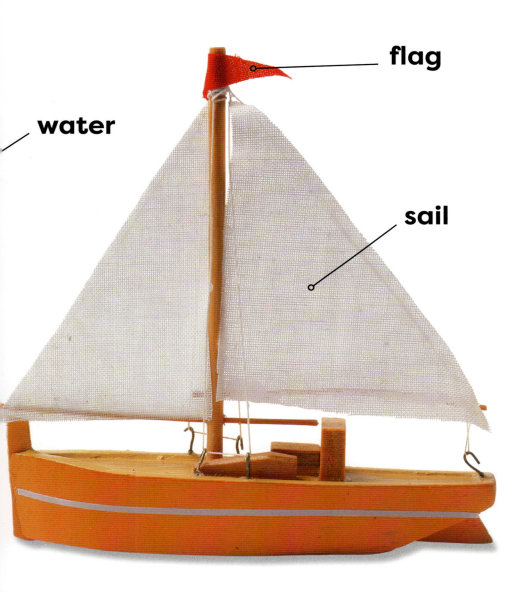

We climb at the playground.

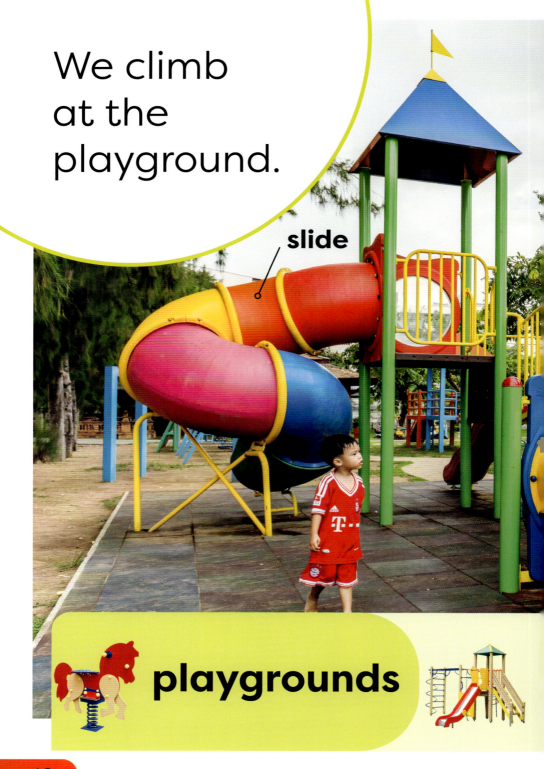

slide

playgrounds

tunnel

swings

We play on the swings.

chains

seat

We run and run with our dogs.

 dogs

ear

head

We ride our bicycles through the grass.

 bicycles

We roll along on our inline skates.

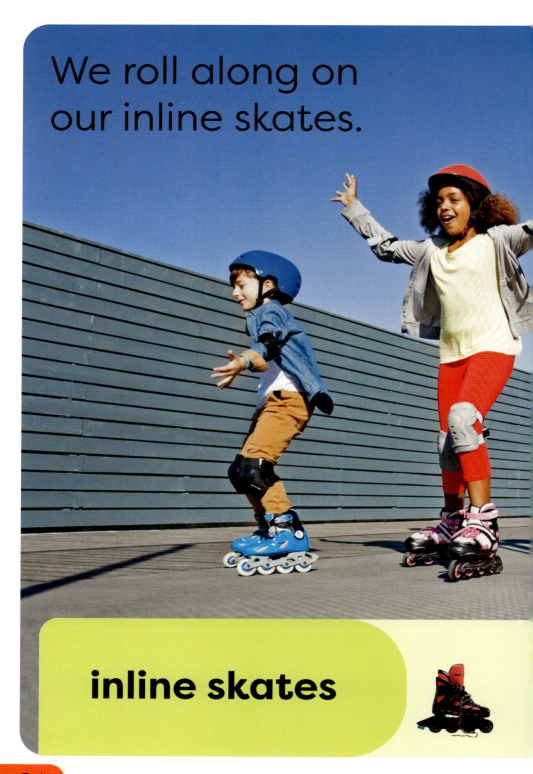

inline skates

We play a game of hide-and-seek.

hide-and-seek

We watch squirrels gather nuts.

The park is lots of fun!

What do you like to do best?

Glossary

bicycle
a vehicle with two wheels turned by pedals

boat
a craft that floats on water

kite
a toy that can be flown in the wind

inline skate
a shoe with a line of wheels on the bottom

swing
a seat held up with ropes or chains

Quiz

Answer the questions to see what you have learned. Check your answers with an adult.

1. What do kids fly in the sky?
2. What do kids ride through the grass?
3. What do kids do by the pond?
4. What do kids do on playgrounds?
5. Tell a story about a time you went to the park. What did you see? What did you do?

1. Kites 2. Their bicycles 3. Watch ducks and sail boats
4. They go down slides or crawl through tunnels
5. Answers will vary